low.

The Making of a Champion

A World-Class Gymnast

Lloyd Readhead

www.heinemann.co.uk/library
Visit our website to find out more information about **Heinemann Library** books.

To order:
☎ Phone 44 (0) 1865 888066
🖹 Send a fax to 44 (0) 1865 314091
🖥 Visit the Heinemann Bookshop at www.heinemann.co.uk/library to browse our catalogue and order online.

First published in Great Britain by Heinemann Library, Halley Court, Jordan Hill, Oxford OX2 8EJ, part of Harcourt Education. Heinemann is a registered trademark of Harcourt Education Ltd.

Editorial: Andrew Farrow and Dan Nunn
Design: David Poole and Geoff Ward
Illustrations: Geoff Ward
Picture Research: Rebecca Sodergren, Melissa Allison and Fiona Orbell
Production: Duncan Gilbert

Originated by Ambassador Litho Ltd
Printed in China by WKT Company Limited

ISBN 0 431 18924 2
08 07 06 05 04
10 9 8 7 6 5 4 3 2 1

British Library Cataloguing in Publication Data
Lloyd, Readhead
A World-Class Gymnast - (The Making of a Champion)
1. Gymnastics - Juvenile literature
2. Gymnastics - Training - Juvenile literature
I. Title
796.4'4
A full catalogue record for this book is available from the British Library.

Acknowledgements
The publishers would like to thank the following for permission to reproduce photographs:

Corbis pp. **5 top** (Photo & Co./Tim de Waele), **12** (TempSport), **16** (Reuters), **22**, **34** (Curtis/Strauss), **40** (NewSport); Eileen Langsley pp. **4**, **5 bottom**, **6**, **7 top**, **8**, **9 top**, **10**, **11**, **13 top**, **13 bottom**, **17**, **18**, **19 top**, **19 bottom**, **20**, **21 bottom**, **23 left**, **23 right**, **24**, **25 top**, **25 bottom**, **26 top**, **26 bottom**, **27**, **28**, **29 top**, **29 bottom**, **31 top**, **39**, **43 top**; EMPICS p. **42** (Tony Marshall); Getty Images p. **9 bottom** (AFP); Harcourt Education Ltd/Gareth Boden pp. **7 bottom**, **14**, **21 top**, **30**, **31 bottom**, **32**, **33**, **36**, **37**, **41**; Reuters p. **35** (Chien-Min Chung); Steve Lange p. **43 bottom**.

Cover photograph reproduced with permission of PA Photos/EPA.

Every effort has been made to contact copyright holders of any material reproduced in this book. Any omissions will be rectified in subsequent printings if notice is given to the publishers.

Contents

Words printed in bold letters, **like these**, are explained in the Glossary.

Introducing gymnastics

The high levels of physical fitness, the daring and technical skills of top gymnasts have thrilled audiences around the world for decades. As a result, the dedication and commitment of the best gymnasts to their sport can bring them many rewards. They travel the globe to compete in competitions, and success often brings them fame and opens the door to opportunities in advertising and television.

After performing a daring somersault over the bar, Ivan Ivankov of Belarus gets ready to re-catch it. Gymnasts practise this tricky movement hundreds of times before they are ready to perform it at competition level.

Sell-out spectator sports

There are many forms of gymnastics but the most popular are men's and women's artistic gymnastics. These two disciplines are the first to sell out spectator tickets for the Olympic Games and more people tune in to watch these on television than any of the other Olympic competitions. Whether at home or in the actual venues, spectators enjoy watching the gymnasts display their amazing skills on a variety of equipment, or apparatus, in both the team and individual events. It is this variety that makes the sport so attractive to watch.

Men's and women's disciplines

In women's artistic, female gymnasts perform dramatic somersaults from the vault, exciting acrobatics on the beam, graceful musical routines on the floor, and swings and twists from and on the bars. Men's artistic gymnastics showcases six demanding apparatus. Male gymnasts show strength and agility in their floor **routines**, complex and speedy hand movements on the pommel horse, balance and strength on the rings, power on the vault and great skill on both the parallel and horizontal bars. We'll find out more about these exciting and challenging pieces of apparatus later in the book.

A big shock

No one expected much from the USA Women's team at the 2003 World Championships. Coaches had been forced to replace three of the team during the build-up to the competition. Despite this setback the USA went on to win the team gold medal. And it was one of the replacement gymnasts, teenager Chellsie Memmel, who tied for the gold medal on the uneven bars with fellow team member Hollie Vise. Memmel remembers: 'It was a big shock to learn I was competing here... I tried not to think about anyone else. I wasn't thinking about the all around at all. I was focused on the team.'

Feng Jing from China performs a Stalder circle – one of the most popular movements of the horizontal bar event. The movement involves swinging a backward circle while holding the legs in a V-shape, called a straddled position.

How the sport has changed

In ancient Greece, gymnastic exercises such as jumping and acrobatics were a hugely popular way for both men and women to keep fit. The Romans developed gymnastics into a more formal sport, but as the Roman Empire declined so did gymnastics. Then, in the 1800s, interest in gymnastics revived again in Europe and spread to the USA and the rest of the world. It has been a major world sport since men's gymnastics was included in the first modern Olympic Games in Athens, Greece in 1896. Women gymnasts began to compete in the Games from 1928.

The 1950s and 1960s

Up until the 1950s and 1960s, gymnastics remained mostly a male sport and strength was a key feature. The top gymnasts were from the Soviet Union and Japan. Famous gymnasts such as Switzerland's Joseph Stalder and Japan's Yukio Endo left their mark when they performed brand new movements they devised themselves. These movements were named after them and are still performed today.

The remarkable 1970s

There were some remarkable developments in the 1970s, most notably the introduction of the release and catch **elements** on the horizontal bar and asymmetric bars. These require fast swings from which the gymnast releases the bar, performs a somersault and then re-catches the bar. Some popular and difficult movements are named after the gymnasts who first performed them, such as the Tkatchev performed by Alexander Tkatchev (see page 24) and the Gienger Salto by Eberhard Gienger (see page 25).

Alexander Beresch of the Ukraine performs a Kovacs from the horizontal bar. In this movement the gymnast releases the bar and does a somersault in the air before re-catching it at great speed. Sadly, Alexander died in a car crash in February 2004.

Much younger gym stars

As gymnastic techniques developed, countries like the Soviet Union and Romania began to select young children to attend special sport schools. There, children learned difficult gymnastics movements from an early age. By the late 1970s, teenage world champions began to appear, particularly in women's gymnastics. Young gymnasts such as Olga Korbut, Anna Pavlova and Nadia Comaneci became superstars. However, there was concern that hard training so young could be harming the gymnasts' bodies. In 1997 the International Gymnastics Federation introduced a minimum age of 16 for major events, and now greater numbers of older female gymnasts are competing at the highest levels.

Young children are naturally fit and are more easily able to perform many of the moves required by women's gymnastics than older competitors. Here, Anna Pavlova of Russia is in mid-air while doing a perfect leap on the beam.

New apparatus

One of the most important developments in gymnastics has been the foam-filled landing pit. Between 1.5 and 2 metres deep, and filled with pieces of fire-resistant foam, the pits make the learning of dangerous skills much safer because gymnasts can land in a soft foam area, rather than being caught by their coach. Improvements in the apparatus have also made it possible for gymnasts to perform more complex movements in competitions safely.

Champion qualities

Champion gymnasts such as Romania's Andreea Raducan, Russia's Svetlana Khorkina and the USA's Paul Hamm and Carly Patterson have many similar qualities. Each of these gymnasts' skills have been developed through hard training and good coaching but, like all top gymnasts, they also need a high level of natural ability.

Natural talent

Top gymnasts are born with a natural talent for their sport. They may be naturally very strong, have great **flexibility**, be dynamic (they can move and turn fast) or simply have more **stamina** than other people. These are all skills that gymnasts need.

Good flexibility is essential for learning moves. It reduces the risk of injury and allows high quality movements to be performed. Amazing strength is also vital. There are many forms of strength, and the ability to perform powerful movements or hold demanding **static** positions requires hours of strength training.

Gymnasts also need to be aware of their bodies when somersaulting or twisting, and to have cat-like instincts that enable them to land safely – we say they have **spatial awareness**. Finally, top gymnasts display great courage and rarely show fear of falling or failing.

Li Xiaopeng

Li Xiaopeng from China has great natural talent and performs with tremendous skill. Like all great gymnasts, he makes difficult skills look easy. He is renowned for his stylish work on parallel bars and vault and he became the world champion in these two events in 2003. Here he is pictured stunning audiences with a performance on the parallel bars.

Commitment to hard work

Natural talent is a great gift but it must be supported by dedication and hard work. A lazy gymnast will not succeed, no matter how talented they are. Coaches help by designing training programmes that challenge a gymnast's dedication and forces him or her to work hard. Success breeds confidence, but self-confidence can also be improved through good coaching. Many gymnasts work with a sports **psychologist** to become confident and mentally tough.

Allana Slater is a top Australian gymnast who led her team in great style to take the bronze medal at the 2003 World Championships. This was Australia's first team medal at a World Championships event.

Craig Heap from Great Britain has good spatial awareness. The ability to perform complex movements, such as somersaults with twists, can be improved by training on the trampoline. This allows the skills to be developed in stages, and improves the gymnast's awareness whilst in the air.

Key qualities fact

According to many coaches, the qualities that separate the best gymnasts from the rest are:

- a commitment to and a love for the sport
- dedication and hard work
- self belief
- courage
- daring to be different
- not being afraid of being the best
- natural talent.

People behind the gymnast

Gymnastics is a complex and demanding sport and a gymnast cannot practise it safely or successfully without the support of many people. Gymnasts usually start training at a young age and compete at the highest levels between the age of 16 to around 30 years old. During this time the gymnast grows from a young child through to an adult, and their changing needs are provided for by a whole team of people.

Parents and family

A young gymnast may train for about eight to ten hours per week. Parents often give up their own time to take the gymnast to training, and there are also training fees to be paid, often thousands of pounds or dollars a year. Without their family's support, most young gymnasts would never be able to participate in the sport.

School and college

As young gymnasts get older they learn more skills and need greater levels of fitness. This means they need to spend more and more time in the gym. It can be tricky fitting a busy training schedule around the demands of school and homework. Many gymnasts train in the morning before school and again after the school day is over. Some schools and colleges provide a flexible timetable to enable gymnasts to fit their training around their education.

Training with friends can provide young gymnasts with support and encouragement.

Support from clubs

Gymnastics clubs and teammates play an important part in a gymnast's career. The club provides training facilities while teammates at the club become close friends. The club is a good place to train safely, and helps the gymnast to enjoy their early years. Attending a club also gives young gymnasts opportunities to compete in local and national events.

Clubs have the facilities that young gymnasts need to train safely. This young gymnast is 'chalking up' – rubbing chalk into her hands to help her grip the bars firmly and reduce the risk of slipping off.

National governing bodies

National governing bodies provide a range of training and services that help gymnasts achieve their best. They train and supply qualified coaches and provide good practice guidelines, which coaches and officials must follow. They also provide back-up support staff such as doctors, **physiotherapists**, sports **psychologists** and **choreographers**. Young gymnasts can attend training camps run by the governing bodies, and there are also national and international events organized throughout the year.

World governing body facts

The world governing body for gymnastics is the International Gymnastics Federation (FIG). The FIG makes all the rules for competition and trains the judges that judge the major events. It also allocates the World Championships to a host nation. National governing bodies must be members of the FIG for their gymnasts to compete at the World Championships and in Olympic events.

Foundation skills

There are a number of basic gymnastics skills that gymnasts use as the foundation for many more complex movements. Even the best gymnasts regularly practise these skills to ensure that they can perform them perfectly each time and to develop fitness and strength.

Basic skills such as handstands practised during training can play a big part in major international competitions. Here, Aleksei Nemov of Russia is pictured performing an inverted cross on the rings while competing in the men's individual event at the Atlanta 1996 Olympics in the USA.

Handstand

US gymnast Blaine Wilson thinks handstands are one of the most important skills a gymnast can master. He says, 'A handstand is one of the most basic things you can do in gymnastics… the better the handstand that you have, the easier the rest of the routine is.' The handstand position can be demonstrated on a number of pieces of gymnastic equipment. It can also be combined with good shoulder **flexibility** to allow many interesting movements to be performed.

Hip flexibility

In modern gymnastics, flexibility in the hips is extremely important. Good hip flexibility allows a gymnast to learn skills more quickly without the risk of injury, and also helps them to show better style and quality in their performance.

The splits

The splits can be performed in the forward or sideways position or together with a body fold. To develop the splits, the coach will introduce various stretching exercises at a young age. These are designed to stretch the hamstrings on the upper back leg and the quadracepts and hip flexers on the front of the legs and hips.

Imaginative routines

Kyle Shewfelt of Canada is a world-class gymnast in the floor exercise. He is shown here performing a forward split position. Shewfelt won bronze medals for the floor exercise and vault at the 2003 World Championships. He is very popular with spectators and some judges believe he should receive more recognition for his imaginative routines, which often include unusual combinations of tumbles.

Dance and expression

Female gymnasts spend a great deal of time learning classical dance movements. This helps in the floor exercise and beam routines. Dance teachers and **choreographers** link dance movements with intricate arm and hand gestures to allow the gymnast to express their personality through their movements.

Ludmilla Ejova from Russia is a dynamic and very expressive gymnast, as she demonstrates here during a dance movement in a floor exercise.

More foundation skills

The best gymnasts in the world can make even the most difficult gymnastics **elements** look graceful and easy. This is because they have mastered the basic skills that can be built upon to produce the advanced elements. Some more of these important foundation skills are shown below.

The lift to handstand

The straddle or stoop (legs together) lift to handstand is an important skill in men's and women's gymnastics and is often performed on floor exercises, pommel horse (side horse), beam, rings and parallel bars. The element requires good hip and shoulder **flexibility** and strong lower back muscles.

The 'swim round' exercise (see photos below) helps gymnasts to perform this manoeuvre by using good technique rather than brute strength. The exercise closely follows the correct hip and leg movements, which ensure that good technique is used in the lift to handstand.

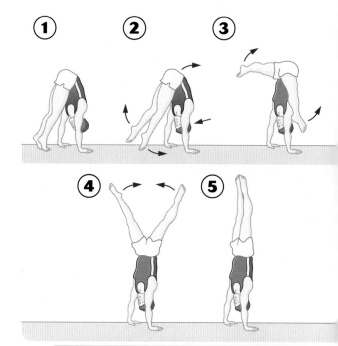

This illustration shows how a lift to handstand is performed with ease and good technique.

This sequence of photographs shows a gymnast doing the 'swim round' exercise, which helps gymnasts develop the flexibility necessary for the lift to handstand manoeuvre.

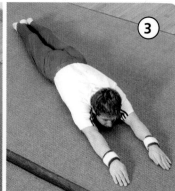

The backflip or backward handspring

The **backflip** movement (right) allows the gymnast to go backwards faster. The gymnast learns this movement as a single element before learning to combine two, three or more backflips to develop acceleration. A run and jump into a round off (a half turn through a handstand) is usually performed before the backflip. This combination allows height and rotation to be created in backward somersaults.

This illustration shows how to do a backflip.

This illustration shows how a handspring vault is performed.

The handspring vault

The handspring vault skill (left) is the basis of most of the advanced vaults. It develops the run up, hurdle step onto the board, take off, flight onto the platform, thrust from the hands, flight from the hands and controlled landing. The handspring to back-lie on a platform is a common movement, which allows the gymnast to develop good technique without needing to worry about the landing. This is because the gymnast ends up lying on their back on a padded surface.

Once the basic vault has been mastered the gymnast may learn to add a twist onto the platform or in the flight from the hands. The very best gymnasts perform up to two and a half somersaults in the second flight.

The backward somersault

The backward somersault (left) is a basic skill that is used by many gymnasts as a foundation movement on floor exercise, vault, beam, rings, parallel bars and horizontal bar.

This illustration shows how a backward somersault is performed in the tucked position.

Women's artistic gymnastics

Before an international competition, a top gymnast spends months working with their coach, a **choreographer** and an international judge to develop **routines** that not only reflect their personality and skills, but also follow the strict competition guidelines. In women's artistic gymnastics, athletes must include a certain number of specific moves on each of the four pieces of apparatus: the uneven bars, beam, floor and vault.

Basic scoring

In gymnastic competitions, judges award points on a scale of 1 to 10 to each gymnast for the content of their routine. A score of 10 would be a perfect score and is known as the start value. Gymnasts then lose marks for missing out specific moves, known as **value movements** and **special requirements**, or for making mistakes. Gymnasts can win extra or bonus points, which are known as additive value, for doing difficult movements and difficult combinations of skills – such as D, E and Super E movements (see 'Graded movements' box, opposite).

Balance beam

The balance beam routine must not exceed a maximum time of 90 seconds. The gymnast may use a springboard to mount the beam and they may mount from either the side or the end. The six special requirements for beam are:

- an **acrobatic connection** consisting of two flighted elements, usually two somersaults linked together
- two **elements** of dance or dance acrobatics
- a turn of minimum 360°
- a leap or jump of 180° with split legs (the legs apart)
- one balance held for a minimum of 2 seconds
- a **dismount** (minimum C value).

The beam requires great courage and good balance and is considered by many experts to be the most difficult apparatus in women's gymnastics.

US gymnast Hollie Vise performs her routine on the beam during the women's team finals at the 2003 World Championships. Hollie was almost disqualified when she forgot to attach her competitor's number to her leotard. Luckily, the team were able to attach a makeshift number just in time.

Uneven bars

The uneven bars, or asymmetric bars, consist of a top bar 2.4 metres from the ground and a lower bar 1.6 metres from the ground. Gymnasts run up and bounce from a springboard to mount the bars. In a competition, rules state that gymnasts must perform a continuous routine without stops. There are six special requirements for this apparatus, and these are:

- a movement from the low bar to the high bar
- a movement from the high bar to the low bar
- a release and catch element
- one element on the low bar
- an element where the gymnast circles (turns round) one of the bars
- a dismount (minimum C value).

Khorkina the champion

Svetlana Khorkina from Russia is a tall and elegant gymnast, who is always a contender for a gold medal. Svetlana has a particular flair for the asymmetric bars (pictured), and this is her most successful apparatus. She became the world champion for the third time at the 2003 World Championships. This was the first time a gymnast had won the World **all around** title three times.

Women's floor and vault

The women's floor and vault exercises are two of the most spectacular events in women's artistic gymnastics. Audiences love the dance-like movements and the lively music of the floor **routines** and they are gripped by the speed and athletic power of gymnasts somersaulting from the vault.

Floor exercise

The floor exercise is most audiences' favourite event and people usually start clapping as soon as the musical accompaniment begins. Each gymnast performs a 90-second routine that can include leaps, pirouettes in the air, somersaults and ballet-like dance **elements**. They are penalized 0.1 off their mark if they step out of the floor area, which measures exactly 12 square metres.

Gymnasts have to match their movements with the rhythm and timing of their music, which they choose to suit their personality and style of gymnastics. For example Svetlena Khorkina, a tall elegant gymnast, uses classical music to emphasize her graceful movements. A more dynamic, tumbling gymnast might prefer to use faster, more aggresive music.

The **special requirements** are:

- one acrobatics series (at least two flighted elements joined together without a hesitation or pause between them)
- a second acrobatics series with two somersaults
- three different somersaults during the course of the exercise
- one dance turn on one leg
- a two-leap connection from a one leg take off
- a **dismount** (minimum C value).

Floor exercise fact

The music for a gymnast's floor routine may be played on a single instrument or a full orchestra, but voices or singing are not allowed.

American gymnast Dominique Dawes performs a dynamic leap during a floor exercise.

The vault

The vault is a solid table or platform with a padded and sprung top. Gymnasts usually perform one or two vaults depending on the competition. They take a run-up of about 20 metres, then jump onto the horse headfirst using both hands to spring off the vault. In the air they perform intricate twists and somersaults before landing on a mat on the other side.

Vault fact

The vault is judged from the point of take off from the board. Judges consider:
- the difficulty value of the vault (called the **tariff**) – the more difficult vaults get a higher mark
- the flight onto the vault
- the flight from the horse
- the landing.

Katie Heenan from the USA shows perfect poise and position in the middle of a vault exercise.

The judges

Two panels of judges judge a gymnast's performance. Panel A determines the start value (the maximum value for the routine) based upon the difficulty of the movements and special requirements. Panel B takes away marks for poor performance, such as lack of height in an element, or bent legs or a step on landing.

Men's artistic gymnastics

In men's artistic gymnastics, male gymnasts in the team or individual **all around** events compete on six apparatus. The men's artistic **routines** demonstrate amazing feats of upper body strength and **flexibility**, along with acrobatics and supreme balance and control.

Men's scoring

The vault apparatus has its own set of rules (see page 23). The other five apparatus – the floor exercises, pommel horse (side horse), rings, parallel bars and horizontal bar – are judged according to the start value of the exercise from which the judges then make deductions.

The start value is made up of four A, three B and three C value parts. There are five **special requirements**, which are selected types of movement. Bonus points are added for difficult movements and connections of **elements**. Deductions are made for repetition of elements and poor performance, such as bent legs or poor landings.

Floor exercise

In the floor exercise, the gymnast must use the entire area of the 12 metre squared floor area. The maximum duration of the exercise is 70 seconds. The special requirements are:

- a balance and strength element
- leap, jump, turn or leg circles
- an **acrobatic element** forwards
- an acrobatic element backwards
- an acrobatic element sideways.

The men do not perform floor exercises with music, but they display powerful somersaults, twists, leaps and tumbling combinations that cover the whole floor area. Their movements demonstrate great strength, balance and flexibility.

Marian Dragulescu from Romania is a frequent contender for medals on the floor exercise. He finished 4th at the 2003 World Championships, but has also won medals at the European Championships.

Pommel horse (side horse)

The pommel horse is rather like the vaulting horse but it has two handles (or 'pommels') on the top that are spaced about 45 centimetres apart. By holding, releasing and turning on these pommels, male gymnasts perform a continuous routine of circular and pendulum type swings, complex circle movements and **scissor** movements. Gymnasts try to use all parts of the horse in their routines and need supreme arm strength to hold themselves above the apparatus. The special requirements are:

- single leg circles – scissors
- circles and flairs (circles with straddled legs)
- side and cross support travels, where the gymnast travels along the horse sideways and facing forwards respectively
- circles with turns
- a **dismount**.

A piece of equipment called a training mushroom is used to help young gymnasts learn good swinging technique for the pommel horse.

A master in action

Marius Urzica from Romania is regarded as one of the greatest gymnasts on the pommel, or side horse. Marius has won many gold medals at major events on this apparatus, including the Sydney 2000 Olympics. He performs very difficult movements with such style that he makes it all look easy. He says that he is good on the apparatus because he was naughty in the gym as a small boy. His coach punished him by sending him to practise on the side horse, but he began to improve and eventually ended up enjoying the apparatus!

Men's rings, vault and bars

Each of the men's apparatus has its own physical demands. Some require great strength; others demand intricate skill and courage. Some gymnasts are more suited to the pieces requiring swinging, such as the pommel horse and horizontal bar. More powerful gymnasts may excel on the floor, rings and vault.

Rings

The rings event consists of two parallel rings, 50 centimetres apart, attached to cables that hang down from the ceiling. Gymnasts hold one ring in each hand and perform a series of swing and hold exercises that demand great strength and balance. The special requirements are:

- kip (a movement from a position below the equipment to a position above) and swinging **elements**
- a swing to the handstand position above the rings
- a swing to a strength hold element (see below)
- a strength hold element (where gymnasts holds a position perfectly still for a minimum of 2 seconds)
- a **dismount**.

Horizontal bar

The horizontal bar is perhaps the most spectacular apparatus in men's gymnastics. Gymnasts perform moves around a bar standing 2.75 metres high. They release the bar, perform somersaults and catch the bar again, never touching the bar with any part of their body except the hands. The special requirements are:

- a long hang swing, which is a swing underneath the bar, moving into a handstand
- a flighted element, where the gymnast swings around the bar, performs a somersault over it and then re-catches it
- a close bar element, in which the gymnast turns around the bar with his body folded close to the bar
- a swing around the bar in rotated grasp, where the gymnast grips the bar with his palms facing towards his body
- a dismount with somersaults.

Jordan Jovtchev from Bulgaria excels at elements that require great strength. He won bronze medals on the floor and rings at the 2000 Sydney Olympics, and two gold medals in the same events at the 2001 World Championships.

Parallel bars

The parallel bars consist of two wooden rails on upright supports that are set at the same level. Gymnasts do routines that combine swinging movements with elements where they show great upper arm strength by holding a tricky position perfectly still. Gymnasts may move all the way along the bars as they perform and they also work above and below the bars. The special requirements are:

- a swinging element in support on both bars (swinging above the bars then turning or somersaulting and re-catching)
- a swinging element through upper arm support
- a swinging element through hang (swinging beneath the bars to hold a position above the bars)
- an element demonstrating strength
- a dismount with a somersault.

Gervasio Deferr from Spain displays the great power and speed that has allowed him to become one of the world's great vaulters.

In this picture of Sean Townsend of the USA, you can see how hard a gymnast's upper arm muscles have to work to hold a position on the parallel bars.

The vault

The men's vault is set at a height of 1.35 metres and placed lengthwise to a 25-metre run-up. In the **all around** competition and team events gymnasts only get to perform one vault so it's vital to get it right first time around.

Judges look for clean and powerful movements that combine length and height with one or more rotations and a carefully controlled landing. In the individual event finals, each vault is given a start value according to the difficulty of the vault, with the gymnast aiming to perform two vaults with start values of 10 points.

Spectacular skills

Gymnastics is an exciting sport and top gymnasts perform many spectacular skills. Many gymnastic movements are named after the gymnast who first performed the **element** in a competition. However, these skills are often named differently in different countries.

The Yurchenko vault

The Yurchenko vault was named after Natalia Yurchenko of the Soviet Union, who first performed it. Both male and female gymnasts perform the Yurchenko – a backward handspring followed by one and a half somersaults performed from the hands.

Top gymnasts may add up to two and a half twists in the somersault phase of the vault. More recently a number of the world's best male vaulters have begun adding two and a half somersaults to the Yurchenko vault.

The Tkatchev

The spectacular Tkatchev skill was first performed by Alexander Tkatchev of the former Soviet Union in 1976. The gymnast performs a fast backward giant swing around the bar and then presses strongly against the bar before letting go of it. This causes the bar to bend, creating a strong reaction at the point of release. During the flight the gymnast rotates in a forwards direction as they pass over the bar before re-catching it. The Tkatchev is usually performed straddled or in a **pike** with legs together. Some male gymnasts perform the movement in a stretched position and may even add a full turn.

Lu Xuan from China performs a Tkatchev on the asymmetric bars. Chinese gymnasts are renowned for the very high quality of their bar exercises.

Eugeni Podgorni from Russia performs a neat and high Gienger Salto. The Salto is one of a number of gymnastic movements which are known as 'release and catch' elements.

The Gienger Salto

The Gienger Salto release and catch movement was first performed by Eberhard Gienger on the men's bar. It is now performed by male and female gymnasts. It is a back somersault with a half turn to re-catch the bar. The best gymnasts also add another twist (a full turn) before re-catching the bar.

Release and catch elements facts

The first release and catch elements were performed in 1976. In a release and catch element the gymnast must release the bar, fly through the air and then re-grasp the bar. Most release and catch elements require a somersault to be performed before re-grasping the bar. Some gymnasts perform a twist during the flight, but top gymnasts perform both a somersault and a twist during the flight before re-grasping the bar.

Turning during a handstand was first performed on the floor and on the parallel bars as a full turn – usually called a pirouette. Today, however, gymnasts perform full turns around one arm in spectacular fashion on the bars and parallel bars. Chinese gymnasts are experts in this type of skill, as can be seen in this photograph of Bi Wenjing.

Amazing strength

Top male gymnasts perform some **elements** that require amazing strength. It is often hard to believe that the men can hold such incredible positions – and some even press out of these positions into new moves. It takes many years to develop the strength to even attempt these skills.

Kanukai Jackson of Great Britain demonstrates the cross, a ring exercise that requires considerable strength and skill to perform. In 2001 Jackson suffered a serious knee ligament injury and turned down a highly-paid offer to work in a circus. He recovered to become the Commonwealth all around champion in 2002.

Dimosthenis Tambakos of Greece performs the Maltese cross on the rings. Tambkos ranks among the best in the world in the rings exercise.

The Thomas Flair

Another movement named after the gymnast that first performed it is the Thomas Flair movement. This beautiful element involves the gymnast moving in a circle on the hands while in the splits position. It requires good hip **flexibility** and good upper body strength. The movement offers variety to the pommel horse routine and many other elements can also be introduced while the gymnast is doing the Thomas Flair circle. It was named after US gymnast Kurt Thomas.

Alexei Nemov of Russia performing a Flair circle on the floor. Gymnasts often move into and out of the handstand position within the Flair circle.

Competition fact

Before they compete, gymnasts are usually allowed 30 seconds to **warm up** on each apparatus.

Good coaching

It is rare for a gymnast to grow from an enthusiastic youngster training at a local club to a world champion with the help of just a single coach. Most gymnasts rely on the support of a number of different coaches to guide them through the different levels of training.

A coach for each stage of development

The skills required by a pre-school (or kinder) gym coach, a youth coach and an international performance coach vary a great deal. For example, a pre-school coach must ensure that children have fun while learning simple movements. A youth coach will have to cope with the mood changes and rapid physical changes that occur during the teenage years, and will need to be able to teach many skills, since this is the main period of learning. A coach of international gymnasts will be good at developing high levels of fitness, encouraging self-confidence and teaching very complex skills.

Growth spurts fact

As children develop, there are times when their bones grow more quickly than their muscles. This can reduce their flexibility and make it hard for them to perform certain skills.

Coaches support and move a young gymnast's body to help them learn new movements. A coach's safe handling also gives young gymnasts the confidence to try new skills without the risk of falling.

Coaching qualities

Good coaches always make the safety and welfare of their gymnasts their top priority. They guide gymnasts through a carefully planned training programme to ensure that they learn challenging new movements correctly, each step of the way.

Top coaches are knowledgeable, experienced and well qualified. They keep up-to-date with new training methods, and have a complete understanding of the rules of the sport. They design competition routines that make the most of a gymnast's skills and earn them the highest score they can get.

Good coaches also learn techniques to help gymnasts prepare mentally for competitions so they can do their best on the day of a big event. They become role models for gymnasts, setting personal standards and encouraging hard work and fair play. Most coaches also become great friends to the gymnasts they train, and are often someone to confide in as well as someone to give support and advice.

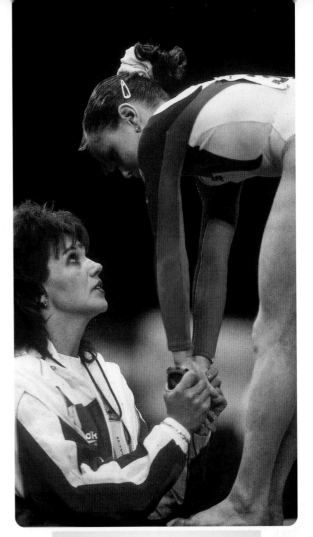

Good coaches know just what to say to encourage a gymnast during a tough competition. Here Elena Zamolodchikova of Russia receives some sound words of advice from her trainer.

A master coach

Leonid Arkayev is recognized as one of gymnastics' greatest ever coaches, and his gymnasts (both male and female) have won team and individual medals at the Olympics and World Championships for more than 30 years. He led the Soviet Union teams to world dominance and, more recently, has been the **mentor** and coach for both the men's and women's Russian teams.

The training gym

In the 1970s most training gyms were very basic, with only one set of each apparatus and some landing mats. One of the most important changes in gymnastics has been the gradual development of modern training centres. The inventiveness of the coaches and design engineers has provided a training environment that is now much safer for gymnasts to learn complex movements.

The modern gym

Today, gymnastics training centres include either foam-filled pitted landing areas or landing areas with sprung or suspended soft landing surfaces. There are usually several sets of equipment and a variety of learning stations and training devices such as the trolley trainer (opposite).

Without this type of facility and quality coaching, it is unlikely that a world-class gymnast could be prepared. Some clubs and regional centres have these facilities, but national centres also provide specialist staff to help the coach.

The modern gymnasium shown above reduces the impact on the gymnast's body caused by repetitive landings. It makes learning difficult elements much easier and safer, and greatly reduces the risk of injury.

Dance training

Top training facilities also include a dance studio. Dance and choreography are essential for the complete development of a gymnast. Dance training mostly involves classical ballet movements, but the choreography is linked together with body shapes, leaps and turns. Dance teachers teach classical ballet skills to develop strength, **posture** and elegance. Both male and female gymnasts benefit from dance training.

This dance teacher is working on ballet skills with a gymnast. Correct posture and limb position are a key feature of a gymnast's training and help the gymnast develop style and elegance.

Training aids facts

Gymnastics movements can be learnt on gymnastics apparatus, but gymnasts risk injuring themselves if they knock into the equipment. Training aids include padded apparatus and cleverly designed equipment like the machine below that reduce the risk of collisions. Gymnasts must repeat movements many times to learn them, and training aids also reduce the impact of this on the gymnast's body. Gymnasts often learn simple or part movements and then join the parts together to develop a full skill. Training aids allow the gymnast to learn each part in a safe situation before putting them together later.

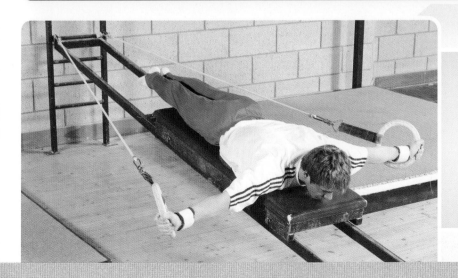

Strength training is very important, particularly in men's gymnastics. Training devices like this one help the gymnast to develop strength through exercises that are less demanding than using the full apparatus.

Learning new skills

Most gymnasts learn new skills at their local gymnasium. This is because modern gyms and the equipment within them are designed to help gymnasts learn new skills as safely as possible. Without such equipment, a gymnast would soon be covered in bumps and bruises caused by accidental falls or collisions.

Learning bar skills safely

Gymnasts can learn the release and catch movements performed on the uneven (assymetric) bars or horizontal bar more safely over a landing pit. With a landing pit, a gymnast can land in a soft landing area before learning to catch the bar. The bar can also be padded, or the gymnast can wear protective pads to avoid hitting the solid bar.

The female gymnast in this picture is practising over a landing pit. The narrow pit and low level apparatus means that a coach can stand close to the gymnast and give additional support if it is required.

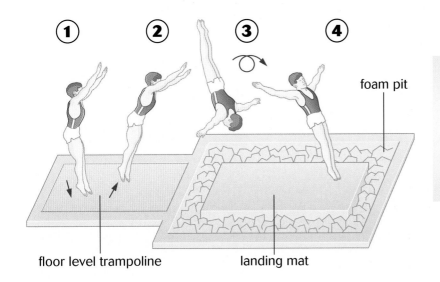

① ② ③ ④

foam pit

floor level trampoline

landing mat

Complex tumbling skills can be learnt safely on a trampoline or on sprung surfaces. This reduces the impact on the gymnast's body and helps them to avoid injuries.

Rotating and twisting

Top gymnasts need to be able to perform single, double and even triple somersaults. They learn to rotate their bodies in a **piked** straight shape and a tucked shape. A tucked somersault rotates faster than a straight body somersault. Champion gymnasts control the speed of rotation by tucking or stretching their bodies, or by raising or lowering their arms.

Twisting or turning around the length of the body is also an important skill. Gymnasts can twist while in contact with the apparatus, but usually they learn to start twisting in the air while performing a somersault. If you watch any top gymnast on TV, see how they control the rate of spin in the twist by wrapping their arms close to their body to spin faster. If they open their arms wide they can slow down the spin.

Gymnasts can learn how to do and control twists and rotations using a suspended swivel support harness like this.

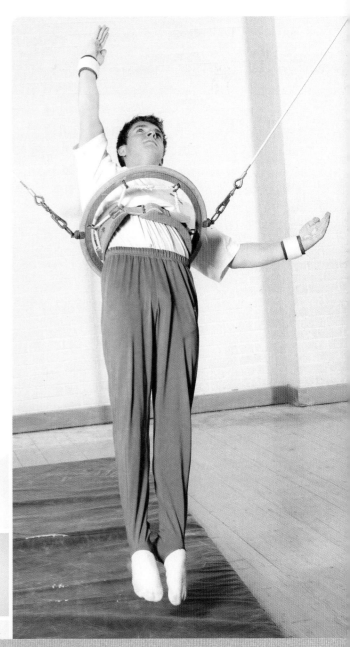

Training programmes

A carefully planned training and competition programme is a vital part of a top gymnast's development. The programme sets out plans for how a gymnast will train and the targets that they should aim to achieve. Coaches try to set targets that motivate a gymnast to work hard, but which are attainable so they get a sense of satisfaction that training is going well. The aim of most training programmes is for the gymnast to reach their peak at a major competition.

A long-term plan

If a training programme builds towards a major event such as the Olympic Games, it may be up to four years long. This is then broken down into four one-year programmes. Each one-year programme is then split into blocks of training, usually around eight weeks long. From these eight-week programmes, weekly and daily workloads are planned. The coach designs the training programme but works with the gymnast to develop the competition **routines**. The coach consults other experts to ensure that the programme is effective. For example, a **psychologist** may advise on confidence and mental preparation, while a fitness expert may help with the physical preparation.

This young gymnast is being guided by his coach during training.

Physical preparation facts

A gymnast requires different types of strength and fitness in order to meet the demands of the sport. The coach ensures that the gymnast trains for:
- general fitness
- strength for particular **elements**
- power and speed
- **flexibility**
- **endurance** and **stamina**
- fitness for practising competition routines
- strength for holding **static** elements.

Technical training

Technical training helps gymnasts perfect basic elements and build up their skills. A good technical training programme is what allows gymnasts to turn single gymnastic elements into complex competition routines. For some gymnasts, technical training involves developing the skills they already have; for others it means learning new skills and elements too. Gymnasts practise these basic skills again and again until they can do them right every time.

Once gymnasts have perfected the basic skills they begin to combine them. They build up a competition routine gradually, only adding new elements when they can perform the others consistently well. Finally, when a gymnast has prepared a full routine, they practise it many times before they are ready to perform it competitively. And even during the later stages of training, gymnasts still keep practising their basic skills in order to keep up their strength for the full routines.

Young gymnasts train on a trampoline at a sports school in Beijing, China.

A gymnast's training record

A gymnast's daily training record is one of the most important parts of his or her training programme. It shows the gymnast how much progress they are making and includes daily training targets and work rates, which motivates the gymnast to work hard.

A TYPICAL DAILY TRAINING RECORD					
NAME: _____			DATE: _____		
APPARATUS	TASK	TARGET	RECORD	SUCCESS	COACH'S COMMENT
VAULT	YURCHENKO VAULT	X 6	✓ ✓ ✗ ✓ ✓ ✗	4/6	GOOD EFFORT
	HANDSPRING FRONT SALTO	X 6	✓ ✓ ✓ ✓ ✓ ✓	6/6	VERY GOOD
A. BARS	FULL ROUTINE	X 4	✓ ✓ ✓ ✗	3/4	GOOD – STAMINA AND CONCENTRATION NEEDED
	FIRST HALF ROUTINE	X 3	✓ ✓ ✓	3/3	VERY GOOD
	SECOND HALF ROUTINE	X 3	✓ ✓ ✗	2/3	GOOD EFFORT
FLOOR	FULL ROUTINE	X 3	✓ ✗ ✓	2/3	GOOD EFFORT – CONCENTRATE ON THE LANDINGS
	DOUBLE BACK SOMERSAULT	X 4	✓ ✓ ✓ ✓	4/4	EXCELLENT, WELL DONE
	DISMOUNT	X 4	✓ ✓ ✓ ✗	3/4	GOOD EFFORT, CONCENTRATION

Fitness exercises

To get the strength and **flexibility** they need to perform their **routines** properly, gymnasts need to do more than practise gymnastic skills again and again – they need to do special fitness training. This is why coaches always build strength and flexibility sessions into their gymnasts' training programmes. As well as being physically prepared, gymnasts need to be mentally prepared for competitions, so coaches also allow time for them to work on their mental ability to deal with the pressure they will feel.

Developing flexibility

Flexibility is the range of movement that a joint has. Good flexibility in all the joints of the body makes skills easier to learn. It is very important for gymnasts to thoroughly **warm up** before attempting any exercises so that they don't get injured. It is also important to practise the exercises with the limbs in the correct position, so that the muscles are stretched in the right direction. Gymnasts should be careful not to force any stretching exercise and should hold their final position for around 20–30 seconds. Once the muscles are relaxed, any discomfort should ease.

Some flexibility training exercises require the help of a coach; others may be practised without assistance.

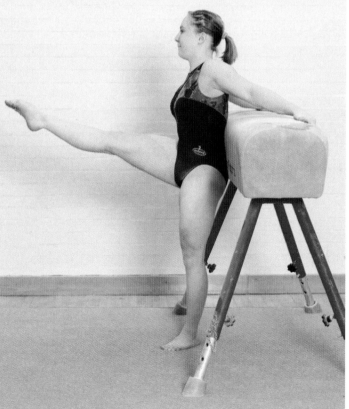

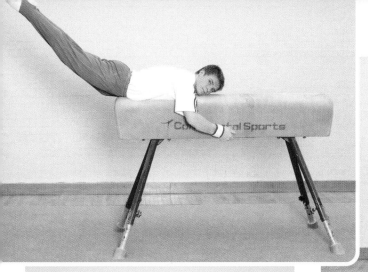

These are two examples of strength training exercises. The gymnast on the right is using a medium resistance exercise to work on his leg strength. The gymnast on the left is performing leg lifts to develop the strength of the legs, bottom and lower back. Exercises like these should only be practised on the advice of a qualified coach.

Strength training

Gymnasts need different types of strength to enable them to train effectively. They need speed strength, static strength for movements that are held, endurance strength for the many repetitions and general all-round body strength. Each type of strength is developed differently by varying the level of **resistance** and the number of times the exercise is repeated.

For all-round body strength, between one and five high resistance exercises are carried out. For speed strength, gymnasts do between six and ten medium resistance exercises. For endurance, between 20 to 30 light exercises are performed. Finally, static strength training usually involves holding a position for five to seven seconds.

Mental training

One of the most important things in a gymnast's make-up is the mental ability to deal with demanding situations. A gymnast must mentally rehearse movements and routines. They try to imagine seeing themselves performing their exercises without mistakes. Gymnasts learn to think positive thoughts, such as 'I can' and 'I will', to improve their confidence. As US gymnast Blaine Wilson once said, 'If you don't think you're as good as everyone else on the floor then you might as well be sitting in the stands.'

A **psychologist** helps the gymnast to practise breathing exercises and develop mind-focusing techniques to help them cope with competition nerves. The coach or psychologist also asks the gymnast to imagine situations that could occur during the event. These sessions help them prepare for events such as a delay, poor scores or music failure so that they know how to deal with a situation without panicking.

Stamina and diet

Another two ingredients that contribute to a gymnast's chance of success are stamina and diet. Stamina is the ability to keep going without running out of energy. This is especially important for a gymnast because losing control in the middle of a tricky movement could result in a nasty injury. For gymnasts, as for all athletes, what they eat can make a real difference to their energy levels and their ability to perform.

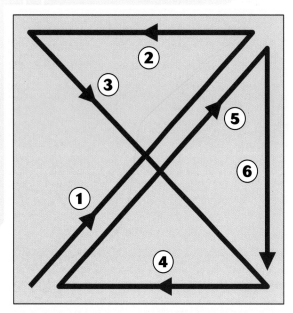

(1) Tumble run

(2) Hopping on left leg

(3) Tumble run

(4) Hopping on right leg

(5) Fast cartwheels

(6) Squat jumps

The diagram above illustrates a typical gymnast's endurance routine.

Recovery facts

- It can take 24 hours for the body to fully recover from heavy exercise.
- Massage can help a gymnast's body to recover.

Working on stamina

One way of building up stamina is through running or jogging. For this reason, many gymnasts run up to 3 kilometres as often as three times a week. Circuit training is also good for building up stamina. Circuit training is a series of different exercises – such as sit-ups, press-ups, skipping and short runs – that are laid out in a circuit with short rest periods in between.

Gymnasts also develop stamina by doing sets of basic gymnastics exercises performed back-to-back, as illustrated in the diagram on the left. These are called **endurance** routines. ('Endurance' is another word for **stamina**.)

Rest and recovery

Gymnasts can become very tired during strength training sessions. It is dangerous to exercise when very tired, as this can lead to accidents. It is vital, therefore, to include rest periods between training sessions. In any case, a gymnast's body must have time to recover and rest, so these recovery breaks are almost as crucial to a gymnast's chances of success as the actual training exercises are!

The gymnast's diet

A top gymnast may train up to three times a day and must regain their energy from the food they eat. The main energy-giving foods are carbohydrates such as pasta, brown rice, wholemeal bread, potatoes (not fried) and fruit. Gymnasts should eat easily digested foods at least one and a half hours before training. A good balanced diet that avoids fatty foods, fast foods and gassy drinks is recommended. The best time to replenish energy supplies after training is within one and a half hours of the end of a session, so liquid energy drinks and energy-giving food are often taken shortly afterwards. If a gymnast has any dietary problems, their coach consults a qualified **dietician** or **nutritionist**.

In addition to eating properly, gymnasts must also drink lots of fluids to avoid becoming **dehydrated**. They usually do this by taking frequent sips of water.

Nadia Comaneci - Romania

Romanian Nadia Comaneci shot to stardom at the 1976 Olympics when she became the first Olympic gymnast ever to score a perfect '10'. Nadia was born in 1961 and started training under Bela and Marta Karolyi at the age of six. Once she had been admitted into their training school, the coaches were able to make sure that Nadia received the best training and was following a suitable diet. She showed such natural talent that Bela soon focused all his attention on preparing Nadia for Olympic stardom.

Drug testing fact

One thing that gymnasts must not make part of their diet is any banned drug. Like competitors in other sports, gymnasts are tested regularly to make sure they are not taking drugs that could artificially enhance (improve) their performance in a competition. Competitors who fail drugs tests can be stripped of their medals and banned from their sport.

Safety and welfare

It is vital that all gymnasts follow some simple rules to ensure they train safely. They should listen carefully to their coach's instructions, never muck about in the gym and always use the equipment properly. It is also best to train when there are other people in a gym so they can look out for each other in case of accidents.

Avoiding injuries

Even though some gymnastics movements might look very dangerous, the actual number of injuries gymnasts suffer is relatively low. Most injuries occur when a gymnast has tired muscles and is losing concentration. Tiredness may mean that a gymnast makes a mistake in their technique, most often in the more demanding exercises or **routines**. They may land incorrectly or fall out of control, and they could collide with the apparatus. The most common injuries are called soft tissue injuries. These include ankle sprains, muscle and tendon strains, or bruising caused by a collision with the apparatus.

Paul Hamm - World Champion

Victory tasted sweet for Paul Hamm in 2003 when he fought off strong challenges from China's Yang Wei and Japan's Hiroyuki Tomita to win the USA's first ever men's **all around** world title. 'It's incredible', he said. 'It's been a dream of mine since I was a little kid.' Two years earlier, Hamm had seemed certain to win the all around gold at the 2001 World Championships, before a hard fall off the horizontal bar on his last rotation blew his chances. These painful memories remained with him in 2003. He recalled, 'Yes, that was going through my mind because I had a disastrous routine, hitting my face.'

Landing correctly

The key to avoiding injuries is to learn to land correctly and safely. Competition rules state that a gymnast must always be in control, and this is clearly seen when he or she lands. Any steps, hops or jumps on landing are penalized by judges. Coaches encourage gymnasts to practise landings through simple drills, such as jumping forwards and backwards, jumping with turns, jumping from platforms and performing somersaults from platforms.

These two photographs show the correct ways to land when a gymnast falls forwards or backwards.

Falling safely

Coaches also train gymnasts through a progression of drills and skills to learn how to save themselves if they fall. When falling forwards gymnasts should turn their hands inwards, gradually bending their arms to absorb the fall and turning their head slightly to the side. They should not lock their elbows, nor turn their hands outwards.

When they fall backwards, gymnasts should point their fingers forwards and bend their arms gradually to absorb the impact. They should not lock their arms or turn their hands backwards. It is important that gymnasts learn to land correctly. Learning some ballet movements is another good way for gymnasts to develop good landing skills, and this also helps to develop strength in their legs.

Coaching facts

Coaches have a code of practice that tells them how they should behave in the gymnasium and how they should treat gymnasts. Key points include:
- Be a role model for behaviour.
- Respect the rights of others.
- Do not bully or humiliate the participants.
- Be caring towards the gymnast.
- The welfare of the gymnast must always come first.

Being a champion gymnast

A world or Olympic champion is a very special gymnast, who has achieved fame and recognition throughout the sporting world. However, the life of a champion is not all about fame, glamour and reward. Getting to the top and staying there can be very hard work!

Working hard

A champion gymnast must spend many hours training, often when other people their age are out having fun with family and friends. Top gymnasts must also spend long periods away from home attending competitions or training camps, and this can be hard on even the most committed and experienced athletes. Finally, gymnasts often work for many years with little financial reward. Training costs money, and finding sponsorship can be hard for all but the most successful gymnasts. Instead, many gymnasts rely on scholarships and grants from their governments via their national gymnastic federation.

Coping with pressure

When preparing for a major event most gymnasts feel the nervous pressure starting to build about two weeks beforehand. Those with the highest expectations feel the greatest pressure. However, most gymnasts have learnt to recognize these feelings and have developed their own strategies to control their level of nervousness. Top gymnasts are better at controlling their state of mind and are more confident.

Beth Tweddle (above) became Great Britain's first female gymnast to win a World Championship medal when she took the bronze medal on the uneven bars at the 2003 World Championships.

Dealing with success

A world or Olympic champion gymnast may face many demands on their time once he or she has reached the top. Television stations and newspapers may wish to interview the champion, who will have to learn how to deal with the media interest. The success of a champion will be celebrated by their home country, and this may lead to more funding support for the gymnast and their sport.

The door to fame and riches from appearances and advertising may be opened. Every other gymnast will admire and envy the champion and will aim to beat them in the next event. This tests the mental strength and skill of the gymnast as they strive to remain number one. Being a champion also brings some responsibilities. Top gymnasts are expected to become role models for younger gymnasts and ambassadors for their country and sport.

Ivan Ivankov from Belarus is a great world champion despite suffering many injury set backs. He led his national team to the World Team title in 2001, and is held in high regard throughout the sport as a superb athlete and a fine example for other gymnasts to follow.

Having to give interviews after competitions is a fact of life for all top gymnasts. Here, US gymnast Courtney Kupets is interviewed after the 2003 US Gymnastics Championships.

Records and landmarks

1896 – The first modern Olympics is held in Athens and includes men's gymnastics.

1948 – Joseph Stalder (Switzerland) performs a straddled circular movement on horizontal bar.

1952 – Helsinki Olympic Games includes the women's artistic **all around** for the first time.

1964 – Sergei Diamidov invents a new move on the parallel bars, a full turn around one arm whilst swinging forwards into a handstand.

1970 – Eizo Kenmotsu (Japan) does the first triple twisting somersault (three turns in one somersault). Mitsuo Tsukahara (Japan) revolutionizes men's vaulting by doing a round off tucked back somersault over the horse.

1972 – Russian gymnast Olga Korbut's revolutionary performances change the style of women's gymnastics at the Olympic Games.

1972 – Round fibreglass bars replace the wooden oval bar in women's gymnastics.

1972 – Zoltan Magyar (Hungary) travels forwards across the length of the horse. The Magyar travel is born.

1975 – Janos Sivado (Hungary) invents the Sivado travel by travelling backwards along the horse.

1975 – Kurt Thomas (USA) splits his legs in a side horse circle and the spectacular Thomas Flair emerges.

1976 – The handspring front somersault vault is introduced by Jorge Roche (Cuba).

1976 – Three release and catch **elements** are performed at the Men's European Championships in Vilnius: the Tkatchev (Alexander Tkatchev), the Deltchev (Stoyan Deltchev) and Gienger Salto (Eberhard Gienger).

1976 – The female gymnast Nadia Comaneci scores a set of perfect 10s. She was the first of a string of great Romanian gymnasts.

1983 – Natalia Yurchenko (Soviet Union) does the first round off and back take off vault.

1986 – The first triple somersault is performed on floor by Valeri Liukin (Soviet Union).

1997 – The FIG introduces minimum ages for female events: Junior, 13 years of age; Senior, 16 years of age.

1997 – The use of compulsory set exercises is abandoned by the FIG and the first voluntary-exercise-only World Championships are held.

2002 – The FIG introduces the World Age Group Programme and Coaching Academy to develop gymnastics in more countries and to standardize the type of skills taught at each stage of development of the gymnasts.

2003 – The American women's team wins their first ever World Team Championships.

2003 - Svetlana Khorkina (Russia) becomes the first gymnast to win three world **all around** champion titles.

2003 - Paul Hamm becomes the first American to win the men's world all around title.

2003 - The Australian women's team gain third place in the team championships to win the country's first team medal at the World Championships.

2003 - Beth Tweddle becomes the first British female to win a world medal, finishing third on uneven bars.

World all around champions

Usually held every two years in between the Olympic cycle, the most recent champions have been:

1993: Birmingham, England
W: Shannon Miller (USA)
M: Vitaly Scherbo (Belarus)

1994: Brisbane, Australia
W: Shannon Miller (USA)
M: Ivan Ivankov (Belarus)

1995: Sabae, Japan
W: Lilia Podkopayeva (Ukraine)
M: Li Xiaoshuang (China)

1997: Lausanne, Switzerland
W: Svetlana Khorkina (Russia)
M: Ivan Ivankov (Belarus)

1999: Tianjin, China
W: Maria Olaru (Romania)
M: Nikolay Krukov (Russia)

2001: Ghent, Belgium
W: Svetlana Khorkina (Russia)
M: Jing Feng (China)

2003: Anaheim, USA
W: Svetlana Khorkina (Russia)
M: Paul Hamm (USA)

Olympic all around champions

The all around champions at the last four Olympic Games are listed below.

1984: Los Angeles, USA
W: Mary Lou Retton (USA)
M: Koji Gushiken (Japan)

1988: Seoul, Korea
W: Elena Shushunova (USSR)
M: Vladimir Artemov (USSR)

1992: Barcelona, Spain
W: Tatiana Gutsu (Ukraine)
M: Vitaly Scherbo (Belarus)

1996: Atlanta, USA
W: Lilia Podkopayeva (Ukraine)
M: Li Xiaoshuang (China)

2000: Sydney, Australia
W: Simona Amanar (Romania)
M: Alexei Nemov (Russia)

Glossary

acrobatic elements
acrobatic elements include rolls, hand support elements with or without flight, and somersaults

all around
competition in which the gymnast competes on all of the apparatus

backflip
backward handspring

choreographer
dance teacher who constructs the dance elements in a floor exercise

dehydrated
when the body does not have enough water

dietician
person trained to advise on the correct food we should eat

dismount
movement performed to end a routine, from the apparatus to landing on the floor

element
single gymnastics movement or skill

endurance
the ability to carry on doing a physical activity for a long time

flexibility
range of movement in a joint

mentor
person who gives you advice

nutritionist
person who is trained to advise on the healthiness of foods

physiotherapist
person who can help to heal or overcome injuries

pike
move in which the body is first bent at the waist and then straightened

posture
shape in which we hold our bodies

psychologist
person trained to help you to become mentally strong

resistance
how hard something is to push or pull

routine
series of elements used in competition, sometimes called the competition exercise

scissors
pommel horse manoeuvre where the gymnast swings with his legs astride the horse. At the height of the swing, he undercuts one leg under the other to swing in the opposite direction.

spatial awareness
ability to know where you are in space when somersaulting or twisting

special requirements
in women's gymnastics, every uneven bars, balance beam or floor exercise should include six different special requirement movements, each valued at 0.2 marks. This amount is deducted for each special requirement not included. Men's gymnastics routines also include special requirements, but the scoring system is slightly different.

stamina
able to do something for a long time

static
not moving

tariff
value given to a movement due to its difficulty

value movements
in women's gymnastics every uneven bars, balance beam or floor exercise should include two A, three B and three C value movements or marks are deducted. There are 0.2 marks deducted for a missing A movement, 0.3 marks for a B movement and 0.5 marks for a C movement.

warm up
perform a series of light exercises to get the body and muscles warm

Resources

Further reading

Most gymnastics federations produce regular gymnastics publications and these include *USA Gymnastics* (produced by USA Gymnastics Federation), *Gymnast Magazine* and *GymNews* (produced by British Gymnastics) and *Australian Gymnast Magazine* (produced by the Australian Gymnastics Federation).

The following books, some of which were written for adults, may also be useful if you can find them at your local library:

British Amateur Gymnastics Association Women's Gymnastics Manual by Colin Still (Springfield Books, 1990)

Gymnastics Skills and Games by Joan Jackman and Bob Currier (A & C Black, 1992)

Men's Gymnastics Coaching Manual by Lloyd Readhead (Crowood Press, 1997)

Olympic Library – Gymnastics by Lloyd Readhead (Heinemann Library, 1996)

Sports Skills – Gymnastics by Norman Barrett and David Jeffries (Hodder Wayland, 1995)

The Fantastic Book of Gymnastics by Lloyd Readhead (Copper Beech Books, 1997)

Websites

Most national gymnastics federations provide good advice and interesting information via their websites. Some useful addresses are:

USA
www.usa-gymnastics.org

UK
www.british-gymnastics.org

Australia
www.gymnastics.org.au

Another useful website is the website of the International Gymnastics Federation. This can be found at: *www.fig-gymnastics.com*

Disclaimer

All the Internet addresses (URLs) given in this book were valid at the time of going to press. However, due to the dynamic nature of the Internet, some addresses may have changed, or sites may have changed or ceased to exist since publication. While the author and Publishers regret any inconvenience this may cause readers, no responsibility for any such changes can be accepted by either the author or the Publishers.

Index

Titles in the *Making of a Champion* series include:

Hardback   0 431 18924 2

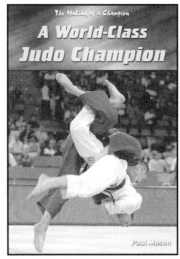

Hardback   0 431 18925 0

Hardback   0 431 18923 4

Hardback   0 431 18926 9

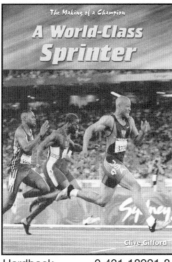

Hardback   0 431 18921 8

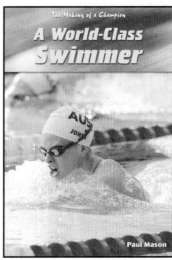

Hardback   0 431 18922 6

Find out about the other Heinemann Library titles on our website www.heinemann.co.uk/library